Monologues
for 'Others'

by Charlie Josephine

∥SAMUEL FRENC

ISBN 978-0-573-13365-7

concordtheatricals.co.uk
concordtheatricals.com

FOR AMATEUR PRODUCTION ENQUIRIES

UNITED KINGDOM AND WORLD
EXCLUDING NORTH AMERICA
licensing@concordtheatricals.co.uk

020-7054-7298

Each title is subject to availability from Concord Theatricals,
depending upon country of performance.

French, an imprint of Concord

USE OF COPYRIGHTED MUSIC

A licence issued by Concord Theatricals to perform this play does not include permission to use the incidental music specified in this publication. In the United Kingdom: Where the place of performance is already licensed by the PERFORMING RIGHT SOCIETY (PRS) a return of the music used must be made to them. If the place of performance is not so licensed then application should be made to PRS for Music (www.prsformusic.com). A separate and additional licence from PHONOGRAPHIC PERFORMANCE LTD (www.ppluk.com) may be needed whenever commercial recordings are used. Outside the United Kingdom: Please contact the appropriate music licensing authority in your territory for the rights to any incidental music.

USE OF COPYRIGHTED THIRD-PARTY MATERIALS

Licensees are solely responsible for obtaining formal written permission from copyright owners to use copyrighted third-party materials (e.g., artworks, logos) in the performance of this play and are strongly cautioned to do so. If no such permission is obtained by the licensee, then the licensee must use only original materials that the licensee owns and controls. Licensees are solely responsible and liable for clearances of all third-party copyrighted materials, and shall indemnify the copyright owners of the play(s) and their licensing agent, Concord Theatricals Ltd., against any costs, expenses, losses and liabilities arising from the use of such copyrighted third-party materials by licensees.

IMPORTANT BILLING AND CREDIT REQUIREMENTS

If you have obtained performance rights to this title, please refer to your licensing agreement for important billing and credit requirements.

THANK-YOUS

Huge thank you to Jonathan Kinnersley at The Agency, for representing me with such care and kindness, and a sense of humour. Thank you to April De Angelis, Bryony Shanahan and Uri Roodner for helping me write my first ever play. Thank you Sarah Dickenson for your dramaturgical brilliance, your fizzy brain and your big heart. Thank you to Sean Holmes, Sophie Melville, Michael Smiley, Simon Stephens, Nadine Rennie, Chris Thorpe and Morgan Lloyd Malcolm for all the coffees and all the words of wisdom and all the love. Thank you to Jessica, for your strong back and soft front. Thank you to all my queer elders for fuelling my courage. And thanks to my mum, for everything.

NOTES ON TEXT

A /.. indicates where a word can't be found, because sometimes words aren't enough, and so the actor expresses something physically instead. This could be a small pedestrian gesture or a big abstract movement. Breath and sound are encouraged.

INTRODUCTION

The first time I encountered the word 'monologue' was when daring myself to apply for drama school. I had to prepare a Classical and a Contemporary monologue, and I didn't know what that meant, or where to begin. I wanted to do Hamlet, obviously. Or Macbeth, or Mercutio! But because I was assigned female at birth, I was told I had to pick a female character's speech. I was seventeen, gender scrambled, working class, neurodiverse, and fucking frustrated. Playing a Shakespearean Queen felt completely ridiculous. I chose Juliet's *'gallop apace'* speech, because I liked the line about cutting out stars. I didn't understand the speech, or the emotional context required to perform it. She felt too 'girly' to me. Which actually is a totally incorrect character assessment, for which I blame Luhrmann more than Shakespeare. It was uncomfortable doing that speech, so to balance the dysphoria I knew I needed something 'punchy' for my Contemporary one. But I couldn't find anything. The local library didn't have much to offer. It looked like there was loads on offer for men, they get all the best parts, all the long speeches, all the juicy words. My mum got bored of my moaning and told me to get on with it, write myself summink to say. So I did. I secretly wrote my Contemporary monologue. And to audition panel after audition panel I said some made-up writer's name had written it, as part of some made-up play that I definitely hadn't seen at my imaginary trip to the Edinburgh Fringe. I lied, again and again. And sometimes the people auditioning me lied back, saying yeah they think they saw that play, yeah it was really good. Which actually is my sneaky top tip for imposter syndrome, tell a lie and watch them lie, cus turns out everyone's winging it.

Anyway, eventually I did get into drama school, and I started writing to give myself parts to play. Because I couldn't find characters like me. And I couldn't bear the pain of that anymore. I needed to be proactive. I needed to learn how to write.

And now I hear that actors are picking bits of *Bitch Boxer*, *Blush* or *Pops* for their auditions speeches! People are using words wot I wrote to get themselves where they wanna be?! It makes me smile so wide! People have been saying for ages that I should put a collection together and so this is it.

This book is for the 'others'. For anyone who's ever felt othered. For us lot. Who deserve celebration and opportunity. I've focused mainly on writing for working-class women and trans people, because that's where my heart is. Class and queerness will forever be an intersecting dance for me. Some of the speeches are from plays I've previously had produced, and some are brand new, daydreamed up just for this book. There is a short description of the character or location before each speech, with some considerations or provocations, for you to use or ignore as you wish. There is also a glossary of themes and tones in the front of the book, so you can quickly look up speeches that give you a specific feeling or context you're looking for. I've written each one with love, with the actor in mind, hoping to provide some juicy material that will showcase your individual talent. I hope you enjoy them, I hope they make your body feel fizzy, I hope they get you all the jobs, I hope your flowers bloom.

Glossary

Poetic: 1, 2, 3, 4, 6, 9, 11, 12, 13, 14, 15, 16, 18, 20, 22, 23, 27, 29, 30
Queer: 1, 2, 6, 12, 14, 17, 18, 22, 23, 25
Urgent and Angry: 1, 4, 9, 12, 21, 27, 29, 30
Soft and Intimate: 2, 13, 16, 23
Confessional: 2, 3, 4, 5, 6, 7, 8, 10, 13, 15, 19, 20, 24, 26, 28
Working Class: 2, 3, 4, 5, 10, 11, 12, 15, 19, 22, 23, 26, 28, 29
Funny: 1, 9, 12, 14, 15, 20, 25, 28, 30
Fizzy and Pingy: 1, 3, 6, 9, 10, 12, 14, 15, 16, 17, 18, 21, 23, 28, 30
Vulnerable: 3, 4, 5, 6, 7, 8, 9, 10, 12, 13, 15, 16, 19, 20, 26, 27, 29
Summink with Bite: 1, 5, 9, 11, 12, 14, 19, 20, 21, 24, 27, 29
Epic: 1, 4, 6, 9, 11, 12, 13, 14, 15, 16, 18, 21, 27
Conversational: 7, 8, 10, 17, 18, 19, 20, 25, 28

1

*(**RABBIT** from* Moon Licks, *written for Royal Welsh College and Paines Plough. Directed by Sean Linnen,* Moon Licks *was first performed at Cardiff's Richard Burton Theatre and London's The Yard Theatre in 2022. Everyone in* Moon Licks *is half-human-half-animal. It's a strange, dystopian world, only eight characters are left, after the day The Rains Came. Rabbit is possibly trans*, definitely queer. They're very sexy, very in their body, they make everyone's head turn. This is the first and only time they've ever spoken in the play. There's flashes of real rage here under the quick torrent of words. They speak confidently and directly to the audience, all during an abstract dance sequence, lights flashing and bass thumping. This speech can be performed by an actor of any gender.)*

RABBIT. I see you, looking at me, thinking you're in charge but, *it's an illusion*! I direct your attention to exactly where I want it. I'm in control. Look. Here. Here. Here. Now here! Now here! Now here! Admire the arch of my foot, my long long legs, my derriere my dear. Oops! Made you look, made you stare. *Look!* Keep your eyes peeled. Don't blink! Or you'll miss it. I walk down the street and I *feel them* looking, I *feel* their eyes on me and *I* control what they see. *Look!*

Light reflects off me, and passes through your Cornea and the Optical Lens, producing a clear image, on a sheet of Photoreceptors called the Retina. The

Retina sends the information, in the form of electrical signals through the Lateral Geniculate Nucleus of the Thalamus to the Primary Visual Cortex, located in the Occipital Lobe in the back of your brain. Your brain then transfers the signal to the Spinal Cord, alllllllll the way down, to your Genitals. Those high high high levels of Testosterone in your blood signal the arteries in your shaft to open. The veins tighten, locking the blood in your cock, causing it to grow enlarged and firm. The skin of the Scrotum is pulled tighter, and the Testes are retracted up against the body. The head of the Erect Penis will swell. The Testicles grow double in size, produce Pre-Ejaculatory Fluid, functioning as a lubricant and an acid neutralizer stain your Calvin Klein's bought on sale last Christmas in TK Maxx.

I, on the other hand, continue to sashay my way down the alleyway, uninterrupted, uninterested, bored. Listen. I've been around the kings, been around the princes, the politicians, the performers, the butchers the bakers the 'can't-help-myself-love's, the vegans the veggies and the carnivores, the 'just-a-little's, and the 'please-give-me-more's, the emperors, the dukes, the bankers in their suits, the west-end wide boys and the east-end gangsters, the northern quarter and the southern hemisphere, the millionaire businessmen and the drunks on your park bench, the clergy and the laymen, the fathers and their sons, the tall the short the long the fat the wide, the boss, the henchmen, the gang, the boys, the lads lads lads, all the lads, I've had *all* the lads looking at me, they *all* look at *me*. And I tell you what, feels the same. They all feel, *exactly*, the same. Nothing special about a single one of them.

So d'you know what? Bring the rain again, I say *bring it*! Bring the rain, bring the thunder, I'll survive it all! I'm powerful, I'm full of power, I'm centre stage and I am *not* afraid!

2

(JAX from Massive *written for Audible, directed by Julia Head, released in 2020. JAX is a nonbinary chef dating Emily, a cis woman. The couple are madly in love, it's all poetry and fireworks. JAX is AFAB and enjoying their masculinity. They're working class and not usually this poetic in public, so this speech is a rare glimpse into their inner world. Performed directly to the audience, whilst Emily is asleep. Enjoy the poetry but avoid indulging in it. Lean into the desire to be understood, the struggle to articulate these huge feelings. This speech could be performed by an actor of any gender.)*

JAX. I think about her mouth. Dream about her tongue. Lose hours deliberatin' perfect proportions of salt, heat, fat, sweat. Want it to be *just right*, you see, I cook for her. Shape up recipes, concoct combinations so exquisite she nearly loses her mind, bring her back down to earth just in time for the next mouthful. I study her taste buds. Learn the sugar chasin' young ones push their way up to the front, eager and impatient. The middle are more mature, craving savoury tones, softer, more mellow, somethin' to savour, to swill, to swim and to sink in. Delicious sinking, aromatic magic, swirl starlight, flowers and thunder, I'm cooking up a storm one spoon at a time. And down the sides? I set 'em alight, spark electricity, zinging and bright and bouncin' up into her cheeks, make her whole face light up grinnin'! A festival of flavour, taste buds havin' a rave up, we started a riot! Pain't each of her teeth with glitter. Spray pain't love letters on the roof. Swing on her tonsils. Bang on her gums a war cry of love, we fought, we conquered, we came! Fill the whole of her mouth with my name! Hear her moan it again, and again! And again and again and again. *Here babes, taste this*, offer you the spoon, watch you chew for clues, how'd I do? What's that flavour doin' for you? Watch you lick your lips, your eyes closed, then suddenly wide, you ask for more and I wanna cry. Seein' I've satisfied you? Inspired you, ignited reactions inside of you? See, I *dream*, of your mouth. Keeps me up *all* night and... alright? Babes, shhh, go back to sleep... And yeah okay, I know I'm punching. She's a queen, and I ain't nearly good enough. But I'm trying. Gonna work all the hours in the restaurant, graft harder than anybody, show her I'm a somebody, but for now it's just her body and mine.

3

(**AMBER** *from* Blue, *winner of the 2018 Bolton Octagon Monologue Prize.* **AMBER** *is a sixteen-year-old schoolgirl. Blue is the feeling she gets when she drinks, or takes drugs. It's a feeling she's chasing.* **AMBER** *is working class and female and trying to find the words to explain huge feelings, so she speaks really quickly. Here she describes a dirty house party and loosing her virginity. Have fun finding the nuance between confessing to us and performing confidence for Callum.)*

AMBER. We spin up the concrete and suddenly we're there, and the house is *packed*. We cram our way through all these strange sweaty bodies pretendin' we're not scared. I charm a couple of tokes off the bigger boys blazin' by the back door, even though I don't really know what I'm doin', I sort of copy them. Swig on someone's vodka pretendin' to like it and as my eyes grow hazy, this smoky sweaty place and that loud low bass boomin' out of someone's speakers suddenly speaks sense to me. My whole body's vibratin' with *Blue*! It's hot, and sweaty and dark, the walls are poundin', like we're stuck in the belly of a beast, the whole house groanin', and I'm just goin' with it. Shitty carpet littered with smashed-up glass and stamped-out fags and cans. I'm lookin' down at my trainers like they're miles away and I realize two things. I'm drunk and I'm dancin'. And I don't know what I'm doing but it feels fuckin' great! The night starts to stutter and skip, it's all bits and pieces, fits and starts. None of it's, linear, none of it neat. My memory snaps in half and whole chunks of the night get swallowed up. Suddenly Callum's there? Suddenly somehow, he's there and, we're dancing? All of a sudden we're in someone's bedroom and I'm smoking out the window like I'm really cool.

"*You're cool*" he goes, like he's surprised. I blush beetroot hot and he smiles. And look, my nervousness wants this to be a slow burn, right? But, well, his kiss is electric! *Boom!* Like, like a match in a cave, and our pace accelerates 'til I'm drunk off his light so bright hurts my eyes can't stay silent. A moan falls out my mouth and into his before I can stop it. His tongue laps it up greedy, hot breath steals mine, our lungs screamin'! He seemed to know what he was doin'. Like he'd done it before. But also like his body was tellin' him what to do? Some kind of animal instinct taking over, deep in his gut, and his groin and his mouth and his hands and his breath, and I was just kind of watchin' him. Spectator to it, I mean it *fascinated* me. Watching his body change? He seemed to like my body a lot, I wasn't sure of it yet, it was new to me. But he seemed to like it, seemed to wanna touch all of me at the same time. And, when it happened, it wasn't quite what I thought it would be. He must have shoved quite hard because suddenly there was this sort of pop and his face changed, like he was lookin' at summink amazin'. And that baffled me cus it was *me* he was lookin' at. Somethin' about me, down there, had made him look at me like I was suddenly incredible. And somehow I managed not to be sick, or cry and push him the fuck off me, hold my hand between my legs until it stopped hurtin' because it *really* hurt, it *really fuckin' hurt*. But I didn't say anythin', I just sort of put up with it, because I think, basically, because of that look. No one had ever looked at me like that before.

4

*(**LUCY** from Skin and Blister, written on the Old Vic 12 scheme in 2019. **LUCY** is working class and hungover. **LUCY** is in a hospital waiting room with her two siblings, the tension has been very high and they're all overtired. **LUCY**'s sharing how she spoke to the married man she's having an affair with. This speech starts off stumbly, then is like a boil bursting. It pours out of her, through her, she gets swept up in it. Afterwards the words ring out in the air, the poetry is surprising to her, the most honest she's ever been. Enjoy the speed of it. It could, I suppose, be performed by an actor of any gender.)*

LUCY. Was just gonna, you know, give it to him straight. Like, right from the heart, be *really* fucking honest. Just, you know, *fuck it*, let it *allllllll* out! Fuck it! So, I said, I said the truth is, mate, the truth. The truth is, fuck it fuck it *fuck it*, the truth is watching you wiv her yeah, hits me like a double-decker bus. Hits me like a double-deck bus WHAM and I'm floored. Flawed to the core infected with this disease, this dis-ease of wantin' wot I shouldn't want. Of chasin' chances to break the rules. Ignorin' warning signs flashin' bright, right in my fuckin' face. Now I'm spittin' up teeth, and shame 'n blood 'n guts, I'm floored. I'm yours. Take whatever part you want. Cus even though I *knew* this was comin'. Considered myself under no illusions and armed with all the facts, the fact is, the impact of hearin' you say Her Name still takes my breath away. See, since we met, my lungs have been behavin' like they want me to die, like they, I can't, it's *hard* to explain yeah, how Hard it's become to Breathe around you. Like my lungs *know*, before I do, that you're no good for me. They attempt to ration the supply of air, tryna trigger that,

Fight or Flight, that animal instinct in me sending me runnin' fuckin' *fightin'* for my life, heart beatin' *hard* cus this heart can't take another beatin' this body can't stand another drownin' in a man and there's *summink* in your eyes, Somethin', in your smile that makes me wanna dive head first no matta how much I know it will hurt and I'm fuckin' sick and tired. *Tired* of hearin' you down the phone, stumble through another *"lots of love"*. Before my thumb saves my tongue the shame of bein' honest. *Lots of love?* I dunno what that means actually, could you Clarify that for me? Cus I'm drownin' over here and I can't tell if that's you throwin' me a life-raft or more fuckin' water. *Lots of love?* Like, I'm your grandma? Prickly chin kisses after obligatory cups of tea 'n cake in a house that smells like cabbage? *Lots of love* like a, like a generic card from Clintons pain'ted prettily I'm not Generic, *We* are not Generic this isn't Clintons, *lots of love?* You, Feel that? You *Feel* lots of love? For who? Not me surely. Lots of love at arm's length in a polite dismissal in a polite refusal in a *Sorry* I just set your world on fire. *Sorry* I just split your 'ead open and poured in a light so *fuckin' Bright* that you see you've been Blind for years *Sorry* I just electrocuted Every Single Nerve in your body you've never felt so Alive *Sorry* I just burst up your heart squeezed every last drop cracked you open *So Wide* spillin' everythin' inside out drippin' 'n splattered on the pavement left pantin' *Fuuuuck*! Sorry I met you, here's a wet wipe, good luck.

5

(**ALEX** *from* Skin and Blister, *written on the Old Vic 12 scheme in 2019.* **ALEX** *is nonbinary. They're in a hospital waiting room with their two sisters. The tension has been very high and they're all overtired. This is the first time* **ALEX** *has ever spoken this honestly in front of their sisters, ever. It shocks everyone. Focus on actively trying to find the words to explain the dream, to avoid the poetry sounding indulgent.*)

ALEX. I have this dream sometimes. Wake up sweating, and cryin' and /.. There's lights in my eyes, in the dream, lights, really bright can't see properly. It's hot and, I'm sweating, and that's embarrassing. I hear this cough and I turn, blinking and out there in the darkness I can sort of see these, shapes, shifting in seats and I know it's Men. Somehow, I know it's men in suits and jeans and workman boots it's Men. Men smoking, men sitting, men Watching. I can't fully see them but I know they are Watching. I look down and I'm standing on a stage? Old-fashioned, wooden. I can't step off the edge or I'll fall. I can't get off the sides someone's, bricked it up? Bricks? Behind me, around me, and in front the drop, and the Men. Watching. And onstage with me are lots of women, lots of, all different, all blinkin' in the lights, trying to pretend we're not sweatin'. We're embarrassed, we hate being Watched, we Hate it, but also there's this like awful sense of /.. Wanting? Like it's a /.. Can Feel their eyes on me and /.. Wanting?! The woman next to me. Then another, one by one are Picked off. A ring flies out of darkness, lands at their feet, hits them in the face, it stings, but they smile and put it on like, relieved? Wearing a ring means you are Watched less, and Ignored more and none of us really want, but it seems like the only, so we All Want, and some make it more obvious. Some, perform, sing or do a little dance, and this doesn't go down well with the others, they get jealous and angry with her, *how dare she fuckin' dance, how Fuckin' Dare She* and she is chosen and /.. *Fuck!* So soon we are all dancing. We are all dancing and it's a difficult dance to get right, the moves keep changing, and my body doesn't, I can't quite. It's hard to not look like you're trying too hard, to look Natural, to not sweat under hot lights. Rings fly out of darkness and we all hold our breath. The pretty ones get picked, the ones that look like they're Good. The Good ones get chosen and the Bad ones don't. And all the time the men Watch, they Watch, All, The Time. Sometimes they shout things, and even if it's Nice it don't feel, Nice, because none of us asked to be here none of us can leave and we are all Tired and Angry, we are Boiling we are Fuckin' Boiling and we are tired, we are tired, we are Tired.

6

*(**EMILY** from* Massive, *written for Audible, directed by Julia Head, released in 2020.* **EMILY** *is an injured dancer, who is dating* **JAX**, *a nobinary chef. The couple are madly in love, it's all poetry and fireworks. Performed directly to the audience, whilst* **JAX** *is out of the room. Enjoy how epic the feelings are, transcendental in colloquial language. This speech can be performed by an actor of any gender.)*

EMILY. I don't know if there is a God. But recently I've been praying a lot. Praising the lord. Thanking Mother Nature, any mystical power, celestial being, the sun or the moon, the stars up above, the goddesses of love. Thank you! Thank you thank you thank you thank you *thank you*! I mean, *fuck*! If there is a God, and it's God that makes humans, then she was surely showing off when she made Jax. Breathing life into that glorious being must have felt like a pleasure, felt like a deep *sigh* of satisfaction and wonder and *awe*! And I dunno why *I* get to be the one to love them. *Fuck?!* God knows why, and I bet you that she cracked a smile orchestrating that introduction. There I was, minding my own business, quietly miserable in my grey little life, then *bam*! In strolls Jax and sets everything alight, like, I'm on fire! I'm literally on fire. I'm a walking down the street or at work or sat on the bus or whatever and I'm *literally on fire* and everyone else around me somehow hasn't noticed?! I'm like, can't you see? Hello?! Why's everyone pretending they've not seen I'm sat next to them like this fireball, literally burning up?! And I know I don't deserve it. That's obvious. I've never exactly been the leading-lady type, I know. I know this is all going to crash and burn into a huge pile of shit and I'll be totally heartbroken. I know it can't last, I'm not *stupid*. Jax has probably just fallen for their version of me, can see I've got, Potential, and is waiting for me to catch up. And I know it can't last, any minute they'll wake up from this weird beer-goggle dream they're in and see the truth and run a fucking mile I know that. But this, right here, feels, it feels, *so, good*. I just wanna keep 'em a little longer. You can't blame a girl for trying.

7

(GIRL FOUR from Flies, written for Boundless Theatre. Flies was written about young women, for young women. It's about hitting puberty and being smacked by the male gaze. This speech was written for a girl, but as we all know, the patriarchy fucks everyone up, so it could actually be performed by an actor of any gender. Really pain't the picture for us.)

GIRL FOUR. My dad took us to see the new *Blade Runner*. I'm not really into that but, my little brother wanted to go and, we only see my dad at weekends and, whatever. I love going to the cinema, share a big box of popcorn, massive thing of Sprite with ice. The film starts and, I've not even seen the first one so I've got no idea what's going on. And it's all sci-fi and gun fights and blowing shit up. My brother is *loving it* he's so excited! Me and my dad keep looking across at him and laughing, his face is so like, *wow* this is *amazing*! Because yeah, who wouldn't want to be Ryan Gosling with a gun, and a cool coat or, Harrison what's his name. Sure, shooting each other and saying cool stuff, great. But. Don't hate me for saying this right, I'm not like, a feminist or whatever, I mean I am but. Not like, you know. Anytwa, I just couldn't help noticing that like. Well. All the women in that film are like, *naked*, like totally naked for *no reason* whatsoever?! Seriously! One of them is literally a robot sex slave who like superimposes herself onto a prostitute so he can fuck her? Oh my god! I was *so embarrassed*! Sat there with my *dad*?! Proper blushing like, *oh my god oh my god oh my god get me out of here*! And then my little brother, he's nine years old, he leans across and I'm thinking oh god oh god what's he gonna say. Cus like I wanna be his big sister you know, be like empowering and inspiring and cool and. He leans over and I'm like oh god, please don't say something embarrassing! And he gets really close to me and he whispers, *Why is she naked?* And I was like, *I don't know.* I don't know.

8

*(**GIRL SIX** from* Flies, *written for Boundless Theatre.* Flies *was written about young women, for young women. It's about hitting puberty and being smacked by the male gaze. This speech was written for a girl, but again – patriarchy! It could actually be performed by any actor who's experienced squirming under the male gaze. Enjoy the confession of it.)*

GIRL SIX. My mum hates her body. Tries her best to teach me to love mine, but she don't love hers so /.. I watch her. Squeeze, and stuff and starve. She don't think I know but I do. And all the time tellin' me to love mine? *Shoulders back*, she says, *stand tall, you're so beautiful!* And I do, though I don't believe a word. Watchin' her mouth makin' these lies, clamp her lips shut, try and stop herself from wanting and wanting and wanting and /.. I *hate* the way she looks at me now. My body's changed. Gone and grown overnight, swelled in places that I don't like you lookin' at, stop it stop lookin' at me, stop it! ...Sorry it's just... I don't like it... My mum doesn't eat bread. She tells me three times that she won't eat the bread, tells the waiter she doesn't eat bread, bread's not good for you, doesn't agree with her, she's not eaten bread in *ages*! And she feels *so much better* without bread in her life and I should stop eating bread too and ooh is it nice? And maybe she'll just have a little bit, just to try, so she tries it, eats half, eats all of it and sits squirming. It's exhausting watching her. Honestly. It's exhausting...what I wanna know is, why boys are allowed to want whatever they want. And girls aren't supposed to want, get shamed for wanting, keep trying every day to not want. Why is it? Why can't I want? What am I meant to do with all this wanting that's inside of me? It's got to go, somewhere, surely? But they don't teach you stuff like that in school. Just maths and science and stupid stuff. School's stupid... I eat bread. I don't care.

9

(CLAY from Sticky, *written for Brit School students, performed at Southwark Playhouse in 2018.* CLAY *is stuck to a TV, until this moment, where there's finally been a powercut, and this is the first time they speak. A stream of consciousness full of anger and hurt and humour. This speech can be performed by an actor of any gender. Enjoy the speed, dare yourself to go faster, to almost lose control as it pours through you.)*

CLAY. Everybody wants to be a somebody. Expressionless faces, all these places, seen it all before. Famine and fucking and fighting and fire and fear. Dead child on the beach. We send our sympathies, apologies, broken heart emojis. Thought and prayers, thoughts and prayers, thoughts and prayers. Breaking news, broken promises. Bags close to our chest. Seen it, seen it all before. Attention please! Public safety, blame shame ignore! Terror, bomb, 400 dead, party balloons, paper clips, burger and chips, three pints of lager and a packet of crisps. Gentrification, intersectionality, anal sex. Gender gap, thigh gap, mind the gap. Tsunami, twitter, terror, tattoos. Austerity, knife attack, hung-over Snapchat. Barbecue, babies, barbies, bitches, BBC, ITV, MTV, FGM, WTF, LOL, ADHD, CBT, ABC, one two three, you and mee. Deep throat, iPhone, broken bones. Adidas, Air Max, there and back. Bisexual, trans-sexual, inter-racial, job centre, David Attenborough, click click click. Tory cunts, gunshots, cumshot, what a shot! Tory cunts, bears repeating, beatings, bastards, ball-bags, blood-bags, body-bags, bus to Brixton. World hunger, world games. Football, terror, Tequila! Massacre, manicure, millionaires. Scandal, cornflakes. Sex on the beach, Ariana Grande, we're sorry for your loss, Our loss, Argos. Thoughts and prayers. Thoughts and Prayers, Thoughts and Prayers, thoughtsandprayersthoughtsandprayersthoughts andprayersthoughtsandprayer sthoughtsandprayers thoughtsandprayerssummer sale, smokey eyes, celebrity, integrity, buy one get one free, everybody, wants to be a somebody. Everybody wants to be a somebody, wants to be known. And *I'm trying*! I'm trying So Hard, to be a person. Likeable, swipe rightable. Re-tweetable, packageable, loveable loved. Trying to do the Right thing. The Cool thing. Cool Cool Cool, I am not Cool. I am not shiny slick screens, metal and dust, I'm not I'm, I'm flesh and blood. I'm fingerprints. I'm, intestines, and pubic hair, and toenails. I'm mistakes and liquid and daydreams. I'm memories. I'm ambition. I'm smells. I'm stardust and skin and ribcage, and piss and shit and bone. I'm blinks and groans and licks. I'm blushes and grumbles and kicks. I'm everything I've ever wanted and nothing at all. I'm taste buds and touch. I'm goosebumps and handshakes, swallows, weak knees, and skipped-beats and breath. I'm electrons, eyelashes, emotions and erections and hunger and longings and laughter and bruises and nerves and neurons and nipples and eyebrows and orgasms and nightmares and appetite and anxiety and sleep and sex and snot and spit and knuckles and fears and ears and wishes and regret and tears and teeth and animal I'm animal! I'm *animal*! And that's fucking terrifying. And also, so, startlingly, beautiful that I /.. I am capable of incredible tragic awful brilliant things. Brutal things. Beautiful things. I'm capable of *so much*. So much that it's /.. I could do anything. *Anything!* The possibilities of today? They're endless, and endless and endless and that's so overwhelming I can't breathe I can't breathe I'm just I'm stuck. I'm stuck. I'm.

10

(AMBER from Blue. Winner of the 2018 Bolton Octagon Monologue Prize. AMBER is a sixteen-year-old schoolgirl. Blue is the feeling she gets when she drinks or takes drugs, a feeling she's chasing. AMBER is working class and female and trying to find the words to explain huge feelings, so she speaks really quickly. Here she describes a conversation with her art teacher, Mr. Davies. Really pain't a picture for us. She wants to be understood, wants you to see it with her. This speech can be performed by an actor of any gender.)

AMBER. Mr Davies smiles and I feel safe for the first time in ages. He goes, *"Have you thought about what you want to do? Career wise?"*

And the urge rises like sap. Belly deep it bubbles up and oozes squidgy truth before I've had half a chance to swallow some back. I want to be an artist. I want to pain't, maybe. Maybe I, I dunno, I know I'm not. /

"You are."

He says.

"You are good enough."

And for some reason I believe him. You see, what I'd done is drawn this whale. This huge massive great whale that come up through London like that one that got stuck in the Thames, like that one but bigger. This huge fuck off whale that swum up the Thames even though she weren't meant to but she don't give a fuck cus she just does what she wants. And she swims up the Thames past Big Ben and the all boats with all the silly tourists tryna take photos with their silly cameras flashin' in front of their silly faces. Grinnin' and oohing and ahhing and missin' all the magic cus they're fiddlin' with their fucking cameras, missin' it all. But it don't matter, she don't pay 'em no breath, don't pay 'em no mind, she don't mind, she just swims past and gets to the steps. Those big concrete cold steps, and she belly flops her way up on 'em, somehow pushes herself up, cus she's strong. And even though her belly's hangin' out all over the place and she ain't really meant to be out the water at all, let alone belly floppin' her way up on the concrete, she does it. She belly flops her way, squelches and squidges her way up over the bridge, water pouring and drippin' off her oily skin, all midnight black and gorgeous. She flops up over the bridge and up through town, all the cars and buses stop to bib their horns. And all the people walking stare, their mouths hangin' open, their eyes poppin', they can't believe it! She's so big and mighty and powerful they daren't go near her, she's so awesome, they just get right out the fuckin' way. She wriggles and glides and belly flops her way up the streets heavin' herself up and forward, one big heavy belly flop at a time, but it don't hurt her cus she's strong and she's been training for this her whole life, she's been waiting for this moment. She makes it all the way up to my school and crashes through the gates and across the tarmac accidently-on-purpose squashin' Mrs. Ketson who's run out screamin' that whales shouldn't be in the playground before the bell's gone, shouldn't be in the playground at all. SQUASH! Squelch and she's flat as a pancake, they have to scrape her up later, scrape her up like a lump of jam. The whale belly flops, beautiful and mighty, up to my window and I climb out and everyone stares, silent, open mouthed and gaspin'. They can't believe I've been picked but I have, I'm picked, me, the whale wants me! And I ride on the whales back all midnight black and gorgeous, back down to the Thames and when we get into the water it's cold and dirty on my trainers, my legs wet up to my knees. We swim out together and the

winds all in my hair and all in my eyes streamin' full
of wonder like I'm cryin', but I'm not, or maybe I am a
little bit. And when we're in the sea, when we're right
far out, she shoots air out her blow hole and I shoot up
into the night sky, and dance a little while I'm up there
with the stars. And then I fall. And falling isn't scary,
it's gorgeous, it's lovely, it feels lovely. I fall down into
the deep blue, splash, and I swim right out. As far as
I fucking want. I just keep going, nothing to stop me.
And I'm happy. The happiest a human being has ever
been. And all the little fishes love me and I love them.
And there's no sharks because they're not allowed, so
it's just me and the whale and the little fishes and the
waves and the stars. And if I get tired, if I get tired and
my arms stop working and my legs stop kicking, then
I'll just float for a bit on my back. Belly up floatin', look
at the stars. And if that gets too tiring I'll let go, I'll just
let go. And sink, really slowly. And it won't be scary
or nothing, sinkin' isn't scary, its gorgeous, it's lovely,
it feels lovely. Like sinkin' into a hot bath, like when
you give in and let him do it, like when you finally fall
asleep. It'll be like that, just lovely. Peace, proper peace.
And I'll sink and I'll drown, but not 'orrible. My lungs
will fill up slowly, but not 'orrible, just lovely, like when
you put a spoon of sugar in your coffee and watch it
meltin'. It'll be like that, just like that.

"Amber?"

Mr Davie's face is frowning. He looks really worried, I
hate that I've made him look worried.

"Is everything okay Amber?"

I say, yes sir, though I'm not really sure it is.

"Why are you crying?"

I say, I'm not, though I think I might be.

"Do you want to tell me anything?"

No sir.

Though I think maybe I just did. Maybe I just did and you weren't listening, why don't anyone listen?

11

*(**JOAN** from* I, Joan, *written for The Globe in 2022, directed by Ilinca Radulian.* **JOAN** *is seventeen years old, AFAB, nonbinary, transmasc. Working class, strong and sweet, tender and brave. Here they're on the battlefield at Orléans. They've been sent by God to lead the French army against the English. Despite the approval of the Dauphin, the men are refusing to let* **JOAN** *lead.* **JOAN** *has been very patient, until now. Enjoy the epic scale of this, it's ancient.)*

JOAN. Hear me, hear me, hear me now! I promise, with every drop of blood in this body, the future history books will bear my name! I'll make it so. Make it impossible not to! Men *will* write about me! And little girls many hundreds of years from today will study me in books. My strength will travel the ages, through the pages she holds. She'll read my words and feel power! Even for just a moment. Men *will* write about me! And no doubt incorrectly. So comfortable writing as men, about men, for other men, these men will cringe and frown at the letters of my name. Grumble their way through scribing my success. Call it a fluke. Call me a freak. Stamp on my grave. For make no mistake I *will* be killed for my courage. Though the source of that be Divine, believe me, I'm incapable of being so brave. My natural disposition, feminine and frail, as taught by all who came before couldn't *possibly* have me on my feet, fighting for France?! And yet, here we are! And here I am! The reluctant messenger, the impossible soldier, God's warrior. Joan!

Wait, let me finish, let me speak!

No?! No. How familiar that word is to me. Two tiny letters, yet such weight.

For you. For anyone here, for whom that exhausting word is familiar. If your ears are intricately intimate with the sound of no, to you I'm saying yes. I'm shouting yes, I'm screaming yes for you. Yes you can, yes you will! There is a voice, deep down inside every single one of us! Somehow we forgot? But it is there, still, it's there for you! And oh if we can just quiet the World for a moment. And listen within. There's a voice guiding you, I promise it's there. It's yours, and yours alone. And until you can hear it, I'll *be* it for you. And if you've lost faith, you can borrow my God. She's big enough for the both of us.

12

(J – This monologue was written as part of the development of the I, Joan *script. It probably won't make it into* The Globe *production, but it's a banging speech so I've shared it here.* J *is transmasc, nonbinary, working class, tender and brave.* J *is on trial, the men are questioning their gender and their god, going round and round.* J *has been very patient but, by now, they've fucking had enough. Enjoy the rare opportunity to speak truth.)*

J. Dictionary's havin' a hard time tryna define me. Bless. Finds it tricky. Flickin' through pages like, *it must be here, somewhere*?! Truth is I'm nowhere. I'm everywhere, all at once. Listen, how mad this is yeah, got *all* them words in your books, and *none* of them fit?! Your words, don't fit. Never been big enough. Twenty-six letters lassooned again and again and still nowhere near capturing me. Too wide, too wild. Your words fail mate, ain't even come close. They're stale male, too slow they gaspin'! Ain't catching me, been hunting for *years* now but *still*, not got a clear shot. They can't get me. Can't pin me down. Can't sum me up in some neat little sentence that trips off your tongue and makes you feel smug. Nah. Put down your pen bruv. You can't review this, can't pin stars on me. Can't rate me, can't pain't me in your pretty words, your words are shit. Listen. They're shit. Like, consistently repetitively disappointingly shit.

Man-made language ain't never been enough. Your binary. Your boxes. Your pathetic attempts to create certain'ty in the chase of illusionary safety. Nothing's certain. Babes, it's allllllll fluid! Sweet 'n sticky, spillin' out your boxes, drippin' all down the sides of your binary. Your girl knows, look, see her blushing lookin' at me. Lickin' her lips, yeah she's enjoyin' this top class workin' class queerness, this premier league boi, this nonbinary finery, I'm a king! Where's my crown? Royalty sounds like our own poetry, I make up and whisper in your girl's ear, when she's mad bored of your prose. When she sneaks out, seeks out, someone like me. Our tongues on fire lappin' up sparks! Her smile's wide got me high like bright skies! Off our nuts on assonance! A verb, raving, in the middle of a noun! This ain't no metaphor! I am fuckin' poetry!

But oh watch them get wild, watch man get mad, this is too much for them! Seriously, the audacity of loving yourself without *their* permission? That's enough to get you killed. White supremacist shit. Basic binary patriarchal society shit. Capitalist you-ain't-enough-til-you-buy-this-shit, shit. Need us small so they feel big, shit. This joyous freedom living-my-best-queer-life shit is too much for them. Criminal justice system was never built for people like me. Shit, said it before but it bears repeating; I will be killed for my courage. The men will burn me. For not being the woman they want. The men will burn me, and the women will watch. They'll make an enemy of me, cus punching down is easier than punching up. And hurt people hurt people. And look I get it, I really do. The hetero-ghetto is wild, and the ladies have gotta keep themselves safe somehow. The Man is too big, so hating on me seems the only available option. The women are angry, and for good reason. But the men saw that anger and had it diverted. Man tricked woman into hating trans. The women are angry about pronouns and toilets and twitter and all the wrong things. The women are angry I abandoned them, they'd rather I abandoned myself. Looking at me and clucking like, *oh but you're so pretty, oh what a shame, what a waste*! I'm not a waste. Listen, I'm not a waste. I'm not a weirdo. I'm not a warning, or a weapon. I'm not a winner. I'm not a wife. I'm not a woman. I'm not a woman. I'm not a woman. I'm a fucking warrior.

13

*(**JOAN** from* I, Joan, *written for The Globe in 2022, directed by Ilinca Radulian.* **JOAN** *is seventeen years old. AFAB, nonbinary, transmasc. Working class, strong and sweet, tender and brave. Here they're alone and depressed following their first defeat on the battlefield at Paris. They've lost touch with their gut instinct and are feeling pretty desperate. Really share it with us, let us in on your insides.)*

JOAN. I was on fire once. My insides alight, divinely inspired, my body burned bright, lit up the whole sky white hot fury and fire! ...As a child, I knew. I was full, of unused fuel. Stuck in my blood. Trapped, under this skin. Latent potential sat patient in my bones, biding its time, waiting for a spark, God lit the match and boom! And oh! How we blazed! ...Now? I am ash. Black crispy cinders. Soot.

*(**JOAN** lifts both hands and speaks to them.)*

Still here? For what purpose?

*(**JOAN** shows us their hands, and waits.)*

I see none... Oh god. Am I mad? Those who surround me tell me so. And yet I feel so sure felt so sure, for in truth the grounds become uneven. I was so certain once. The Truth felt, so true. Untouchable. And yet, somehow, the doubts crept in, found tiny cracks and grew like mould here in the back of my mind. I tried my best to ignore them at first, avoid their gaze and yet they grew. They grew, they grew until I am lost. I am lost, oh god I am /.. My hands shake?! Where once they were still. My stomach twists where once it was calm, my voice trembles where once it commanded an army?! The doubt, whispers at first, found confidence,

found volume, grew deafening until I could not hear
The Voice at all, couldn't hear it, can't hear it, I can't
hear you where I can't where are you where are you?
Am I mad? It all seems so real and yet. /.. Oh god. I
don't know. I don't know, I /.. I never asked for this!
And I never once complained! /.. This is your doing! I
/.. Oh God, forgive me. I am at your mercy. I surrender.
Please, guide me. Please.

14

*(***BILLY*** *from* Birds & Bees, *directed by Rob Watt for Theatre Centre. In response to Covid-19 a film of the play was released to schools as part of a free digital package. The package includes online live workshops, Q&A with the creatives, and eighteen lesson plans for teachers in PSHE, English and Drama. It is free for all state schools in the country. The film was also available for public viewing at Soho Theatre online. A new version of the play will tour schools and theatres nationally in 2023.* ***BILLY*** *is nonbinary and uses they/them pronouns. They're letting rip here, finally speaking the truth.)*

BILLY. The truth, the painful truth, is that this whole thing could have been prevented! If we'd all been better educated. If facts were stated. Not syllabuses written by opinionated politicians? Editing reality, ignoring technology, clinging to some old Christian ideology? Covering a nation in guilt giving voice to the haters glossing over the abuse from ignorant homophobic wasters. Yeah, LGBTQ might sound like alphabet soup unless one of them letters describes you. Then what you gonna do? How you gonna learn that your desires are sane when you're surrounded by silence and hungover hate from Section 28? How are girls meant to 'own their own bodies', when they're shamed for masturbation? Sex Ed focused solely on male ejaculation? Choosing to Edit Out clitoral stimulation? We're all hungry for anatomy edification! Feed us enlightenment! Need us some elevation! Got a whole nation frustrated with fabrications young minds neglected are seriously affected, nah we ain't got time to be patient! Like bears got us bated, baring teeth, overstimulated, yet still you ignore the X-Rated on our mobile phones? Click, swipe, hardcore fornication, with no explanation, no honest communication? Pornography in the pockets of children. And in the classroom? Barely some barebones biology of heterosexual sex. No lessons on consent, or emotions, or pleasure. Over-worked and under-paid teachers are tryna jump through hoops, back-dated and gated, feel jaded, knowing the time will come if we waited when those ill-fated and un-catered for will slip straight through the cracks. Governments painted over facts, turned a blind eye to the essentials, like 'boys will be boys' and that's that? Stiff upper lip British embarrassment blushing and bumbling through the birds and the bees. Got us on our knees begging for clear clarification, no excuses or justifications. We're not some statistics in a government survey. We're real people, let down by a system that's failing. And nah, that's not me playing a blame game, but your shame is getting passed on to us and that's a fact. So what are we gonna do about that?! You really gonna point the finger at Cherrelle and Jack? Young couple sexting, 'let themselves down', and that's that?! Nah, look, teachers, we see you, we know it's grim. Standing up in front of us, trying not to blush, tryna rush through these awkward conversations about sex, cus us rowdy Year Tens ain't making your job any easier let's be honest. Nah we get it, it's tough. And though we've all gotta take the rough with the smooth, we're here to say it's time to change. It's time to change. It's time, to change. So let's make some changes together, yeah?

15

*(***JOAN*** *from* I, Joan, *written for The Globe in 2022, directed by Ilinca Radulian.* **JOAN** *is seventeen years old. AFAB, nonbinary, transmasc. Working class, strong and sweet, tender and brave. They have just convinced the men that they've been sent by God to lead the French army against the English. This is the first time* **JOAN** *has directly addressed the audience. Really let us see you in the fizz of it all.)*

(Once **JOAN** *is sure they're alone, they turn to us and explode into shocked giggles.)*

JOAN. Oh! /.. Oh! /.. Oh God I was *so brave*?! Did you see me?! Did you see?! I was *so brave*! My body, stood, so *still*?! And so *strong*?! And so, *sure*?! Not even the slightest tremor in my hand, no restlessness or unease in my skin no, no breathlessness or, or panicked /.. but standing, *proud*? Like, like I *owned* the very ground I stood upon? Like I deserved to be there, unquestionably, just, *there*. Being heard. They listened! Is this what it is to be a man? And oh! I spoke so well! Did you *hear* the words that poured through me? Beautiful words! And the way my mouth formed the sounds?! I /.. Oh! What honour, what an *honour* it is, to be this, channel. So, so humbled am I to have experienced that, magic! For that, that was not me. I /.. Impossible, completely impossible! And yet, today, just for one moment, I was the place through which the Infinite expressed itself. And express itself, *it did*! Oh, those words?! They poured through me with such clarity and oh, such confidence! Such convincing confidence I, *I* am convincing, *they* are convinced?! Did you see their faces?! ...But, oh, oh no. Oh no this must end here, I can't repeat that I /.. I need to go home. I need to /.. Oh God, please help me, I /.. Surely this is some terrible mistake. Like, of all the vessels to choose from, am I really the best choice?! Not of course that I'm questioning you, I just /.. War? /.. Me? /.. I, Joan, I am to lead, the French Army, into battle? I, little Joan? Are you mad?! ...And yet...I hardly dare say it, but, it's undeniable. This tiny flicker of a flame, deep in my belly that desires this, that believes... Why not I? It is a thing that must be done. And someone must be the one to do it. And the doing of it is more vital than the man who does it, or woman or /.. So why not I? Why not Joan? Joan the warrior?

(**JOAN** *giggles.*)

No! No, come now Joan, be serious. Be serious, very, serious. And stern!

(*They try this on for size. They like it.*)

Yes! And macho! Yes! Yes that's, that's much better I /.. Oh! To prayer Joan, to prayer.

16

*(**FOX** from* Moon Licks, *written for Royal Welsh College and Paines Plough. Directed by Sean Linnen,* Moon Licks *was first performed at Cardiff's Richard Burton Theatre and London's The Yard Theatre in 2022. Everyone in* Moon Licks *is half-human-half-animal. It's a strange, dystopian world, only eight characters are left, after the day The Rains Came.* **FOX** *is hardworking, curious and kind.* **FOX** *is desperately trying to help everyone at all times, and failing spectrally. Here they pause to address the audience and share their story of the day The Rains Came. This speech can be performed by an actor of any gender.)*

FOX. In the beginning, before The Rains Came there was quiet. Quiet quiet. Deep, like, early morning quiet. Cold church quiet. Bottom of the ocean, top of the tallest tree, way out there in the distance quiet. Saying I love you and meaning it quiet. First sip of tea and, ah /.. Settle in the here and now, reach down into the centre where the world is not spinning and drink up this holy peace quiet. This holy peace, this breathe with me, this let things be. Because in that space, that calm, quiet, god-like space, we were perfect. We were loved. We were something divine.

But somehow, we got lost. Got lost in the fear, in the idea that maybe we're not quite enough, and any minute everyone will see, everyone will know and so we threw ourselves into noise. Trying to distract ourselves, buying shit we didn't need, eating food we didnt taste and fucking people for the sake of fucking. We got busy, we got busier, we got busier, we got tired so fucking tired but, we couldn't stop, because we'd all got so proud and the noise was so loud, so fucking loud it got scary. So scary we lost all sense of peace, got lost, knee-deep in noise and lies and broken promises and applause and disappointments and hurts and fuck not enough and thunder and noise and nightmares and fuck busted hearts and dark and noise not enough fuck not enough fuck and noise and noise and noise fuck and noise and she held my face?

She looked at me, and said, I want you to remember you came from the sky.

Said, you're made of stardust.

Said, you deserve to be here.

Then The Rains Came, and all fucking hell broke loose.

17

*(**ACTOR ONE** from* Moon Licks, *written for Royal Welsh College and Paines Plough. Directed by Sean Linnen,* Moon Licks *was first performed at Cardiff's Richard Burton Theatre and London's The Yard Theatre in 2022. Everyone in* Moon Licks *is half-human-half-animal. It's a strange, dystopian world, only eight characters are left, after the day The Rains Came. Sometimes the actors remove their costumes and step out of character to directly address us as actors. This is one of those warm, honest moments of genuine connection with an audience. This speech can be performed by an actor of any gender.)*

ACTOR ONE. I remember the first panto I saw like it was yesterday. I must have been about the same age. And my dad's factory had got these discounted tickets, so it was me and my dad and all the dads from work. And like, looking back I can now see the queerness in it, but of course I didn't know it was that at the time. I don't remember which panto it was, but I remember the baddy. In this tight black costume, with sequins! And a cape! And, this Epic song and dance number about being baaaaaad! And I was like, what, is, this?! Just, something, in the dance? Or the words? Or the vibration in my chest from his singing? And like I knew that it was naughty that it was like, progressive, sexually, somehow, because it was a man dressed as a sort of woman-baddy-type-villain?! This like sexy villain! Ugh! So sexy! And making everyone question their sexuality and like, just filthy adult jokes that I didn't understand but could feel the reverberation of around the room. And I'm there, sneaking glances up at all these macho blokes from my dad's factory who Could,

Not, Take, Their, Eyes Off, this, Fabulous, Demon! Yeah! It was, spectacular! Just. Urgh! And something in me felt, seen, you know?! Before I even understood anything I /.. Like, all of that mental gymnastics that queer people have to do, in order to fit themselves into the story, like, into the protagonists shoes. Like, okay if I squeeze myself in here, and squint a bit, and chop this bit off and ignore that bit and bend myself out of shape then I can almost feel like maybe I just about fit into this storyline?! All of that, mental gymnastics, that I actually think is a superpower, but is obviously exhausting. All of that was gone, for a moment. And I just felt seen. Like, oh! There's someone like me?! I do fit into stories?! There is a character I could play, there's a storyline for me, so maybe I matter too like, my story matters too?!

Yeah. It was cool. And like, looking back, it was probably problematic as fuck now, for like so many reasons but. Still, kinda wonderful.

18

(**FRANKIE** *from* One Of Them Ones, *written for Pentabus Theatre, 2023.* **FRANKIE**, *they/he, is eighteen years old. Nonbinary, transmasc. Working class. Strong and sweet, with wide-eyed wonder.*)

FRANKIE. Doctors all look the same, like getting a PhD changes your face or, I dunno. They make a really big thing about my hair. My skin fade fascinates. Ask me when I first shaved. Like it's significant. Clothes too, seem to make the man. How long have I worn 'boys' clothes'? They don't laugh when I joke that they're not boys clothes, they're mine, I'm no thief. No comedian either by the look on their faces. What about pronouns they ask. And something inside me snaps. And I'm up on the desk screaming I don't want to talk about pronouns! Or clothes! Or hair! I don't want to discuss with you anything about my exterior at all. I want to talk about my wild insides! I want to give you a glimpse of the inky blue depths, the cosmos I hold. I am king! I am mountain! I am something ancient and wise and divine! I am regal. I am proud lion lazing in the sun rolling big bored eyes at your stupid questions! I am both, and neither! I am everything, and nothing. I am oak tree bark. I am ocean spray. I am cold water on hot summer daze. I am strong and tender, brave and afraid. I am soft. I am fierce. I am so unsure of this skin I slink in and at the same time so protective of myself as a matter of fact. As a matter of survival, as a matter of joyous rebellion. I am the revolution. I am I am I am! Are you? I want to say all this, I want to scream it in their faces and write it in their files and pain't it on the walls. But I don't. I nod and smile. Play the game to get the prize I'm here for. I nod, I smile, I grit my teeth. I get put on another waiting list.

19

(**SHARK** *from* Moon Licks, *written for Royal Welsh College and Paines Plough. Directed by Sean Linnen,* Moon Licks *was first performed at Cardiff's Richard Burton Theatre and London's The Yard Theatre in 2022. Everyone in* Moon Licks *is half-human-half-animal. It's a strange, dystopian world, only eight characters are left, after the day The Rains Came.* **SHARK** *is depressed and struggling to stay afloat. They've just upset their partner, Wasp, who has stormed offstage. They spin and catch us watching, and this speech pours out of them. They really ask the questions they ask. This speech can be performed by an actor of any gender.)*

SHARK. What?! Sorry. I just /.. I can't sleep. I've googled it. Someone's done a video explaining how they watch other videos to help them sleep. Makeup tutorials. Men chopping wood. Electrical explanations from engineers. Calm confident voices sharing top tips on really boring topics. Boring is soothing. I try it and have the weirdest dreams. Trees growing out of my ears. I google that but every page has a different explanation and I don't know if I'm dying or lucky or about to feel more motivated? Everyone's into astrology these days. Have you noticed that? Maybe it's cheaper than therapy. I google drowning. I google funeral parlours. It's really expensive. Marble or granite? Cardboard coffins? I google environmentally friendly ways to dispose of a body. I google self care. I can't afford that either. Shiny, middle class patronising, million fucking miles from me and my /.. Fuck! /.. *(Calmly.)* Fuck your self care.

(**SHARK** *watches us for a moment. Closes their eyes, breathes, opens them.)*

The day before The Rains Came, I was on the bus to work. And it was shit. Everything was shit. It all just, everything, felt Shit. And I looked up from my shitty shitness and there was this girl. This little girl, a few seats in front of me, and she's got a slinky. One of them toys, one of them, slinky toys. Rainbow plastic, spiralling round and she was, slinking, it from one hand to the other and she sees me looking. And she looked at me though her slinky, like a telescope like /.. And I winked! I don't know I just, I winked at her I, and she smiled. She smiled and suddenly, suddenly I felt like everything is actually all ok, all ok again. Like maybe there is love? Then she got off the bus, and everything got shit again. So yeah, the day The Rains Came? I welcomed the water. Deep sea me is used to blue, honestly it's true. Being on dry land is the real hard work. I dunno how you lot do it. Takes my breath away, feeling this empty.

20

*(**BIRDIE** from* Moon Licks *written for Royal Welsh College and Paines Plough. Directed by Sean Linnen,* Moon Licks *was first performed at Cardiff's Richard Burton Theatre and London's The Yard Theatre in 2022. Everyone in* Moon Licks *is half-human-half-animal. It's a strange, dystopian world, only eight characters are left, after the day The Rains Came.* **BIRDIE** *is highly strung and selfish, desperate to control in the attempt to feel safe. We see a glimpse of their vulnerability here, underneath all the sassy exterior. This speech can be performed by an actor of any gender.)*

BIRDIE. I stretch, every day. I pray, though I don't believe, I read Important literature every morning. I eat only plants and seeds. I don't engage in negativity. I do what I need to do to stay well. Unlike some of this lot. Some of this lot don't care, don't engage, don't even try. They're stupid. Stupid, filth. Well, they got what was coming to them the day The Rains Came. Washed them all away down the drain and good, I say. I say good! Goodbye! Good riddance! Good old rain, washed them all away! Good old rain will be back if people aren't more careful. I'm careful. I'm good. I put up with all their filth. I put on makeup. I put on perfume. I do my hair like the girls in magazines like the pop stars the movie stars the porn stars I'm a star I'm a star I'm a star I'm /.. I put on high heels. Higher. Higher. I put on tight jeans. Tighter. Tighter, I eat less and run more, smile less and pout more, feel less and look more. I look more I look more I look more like I'm /.. Less like I'm /.. Less like I feel, less /.. I have a confession to make. Now seems as good a time as ever. And, yes, apparently to you Unless you passionately object, no? You'd be honoured? Thought so. You see. And this is Top Secret. The toppest of the top of secrets. Right up there with don't fucking tell anyone ever or you'll die secrets. Don't tell anyone. The truth. You see, the truth. God I can't say it. The truth is. I can't fly. I mean I can, obviously, you've seen but. What I mean is I can't Fly. I can't just let go and, go with the flow and you know, Fly! I mean yes, I can Travel from one place to another. A carefully planned route, that's been checked three times at least for all possible Risks, following the Strict suggestions under the Risk Assessment section of the Health and Safety Regulations set out by the World Organisation of Air Travel. I can Travel, I Travel every day. I'm not talking about Travelling I'm talking about Flying, really Flying. Wind beneath my wings, no purpose or direction or timeframe or rules or regulations no nothing at all just, let go, and Fly! Can't do it. And that makes me a bit /.. You know? Well, that's my sorry little sob story. What about you? Hoping this moon dance thing will do something for you? Get fixed by the eclipse? No? Oh right! Just us birds that are fucked then? Sharks are perfect and living lovely little lives thank you very much! Oh right! Well! Thanks very much.

21

(BECKY from Skin and Blister, *written for the Old Vic 12 Season 2019. BECKY is hardworking and highly strung, trying to survive patriarchy by doing everything right. She's about to snap. BECKY is about to marry Mike, a man she's yet to admit she doesn't love. In this scene, she is ranting at her sister Lucy, who's fucking all the married men in the attempt to play patriarchy at its own game. They're in a hospital waiting room with their nonbinary sibling Alex. Tensions are high, and BECKY has tried to remain calm, but Lucy has pushed one too many buttons, prompting this speech.)*

BECKY. I know you think you're being clever, but you're not. This, Promiscuity? This, 'Power'? Fucking everyone because no one loves you? Doesn't work. In the end it's you that's left alone. Because in this world, they are fucking you, in this world, men fuck and women are fucked. You let them fuck you, so you're fucked! You're fucked! And yes my life is more, Traditional. From the outside, yes, maybe I do look like I'm, playing by the rules. And what's wrong with that? This is the world we live in. Men are in charge and that's never going to change, and the only way women can have any power is if they marry a Good man. That's a fact. That's reality. That's natural, that's the world we live in. I mean, they say behind every good man /.. And I'm Proud to be that women. Mike and me? We're a team. And yes he 'wears the trousers' so to speak, he's the 'man of the house', but really? Behind the scenes? I get to run the home, I get to raise a family. My dream home! I could never achieve that by myself. That, feeling? That sense of Home I get with him? That safety that /.. When I'm in his arms, when I'm his Wife? That ring on my finger means I won't ever have to put up with any Shit ever again. I'm off limits, I'm sorted, I'm Safe. Other men will see the ring and they'll know. Other women see the ring and they'll know that I'm loved. I'm Loved. That ring? Shows I'm worth it, I'm mature enough to be in a healthy relationship. I'm a good women I'm healthy I'm Happy I'm /.. we can't all be like you, using your body? Using sex to get what you want? It's cheap. It's cheating. He'll never love you. He'll never love you, no one will ever respect you. Yes you'll get attention. Yes you'll turn heads. Yes men will Look. But really? We all just think you're a slag! Women like you? The Sexy ones. The Girly ones. The Marylin Monroes. The Kardashians. Fucking Susan! Sexy, so bloody sexy and pretty and Thin all the, all the fucking time?! All of you! We hate you! We fucking Hate you! Pretending to be businesswomen? Pretending to be, artists? Pretending to be Women you're just whores, dirty fucking whores that No one wants No one wants you they just Fuck you, they just Fuck you because they can then they Throw you away! You'll never be loved, never be, Respected never be, just like mum! You're just like her, just the same, and look! Even this, this, Suicide this, So, Fucking, Selfish, you'll Never change you'll always be Alone always be Fucked because you're Broken because you're Dirty you're fucking Dirty they Fuck you then they Leave you they Fuck you then they Leave you they Fuck you then they Leave you they Fuck you then they Leave you they Fuck you then they Leave you to be with Women Like Me. I'm a Good woman. I'm making Choices. I'm making Sacrifices. I'm working Hard I'm working so Fucking Hard and you don't even. It's not about the Cheap thrills or feeling good or Pleasure or even Love I'm marrying a man I don't love. I don't love him! I don't love him! I don't love him. But I am marrying him, because that's what Good women do, that's what, that's, that's what /.. I /.. I /.. Oh, oh god.

22

*(Written just for this collection, for anyone
who's ever been in awe of an elder butch. Call
it* Rebel Dyke *if it needs a title. Shout out
to Joelle Taylor and Veronica Fearon and
Roman Manfredi.)*

Rebel Dyke! She self-claims this title with pride, with
eyes bright, and dirty grin wide. She both terrifies and
soothes you. Startles and moves you, she'll shock and
seduce you. Rebel Dyke. Beautiful butch. My hero.
Makes my stomach flip, and my mouth smile and my
back stand tall, like she taught me to. Rebel Dyke, the
king of every room she struts through, all eyes on her as
she crosses to me, to me? Ruffles my hair, get off! Dirty
laugh, dirty grin. Slurps a pint, wipes her mouth on the
back of her hand. Her hands. Can't take my eyes off her
hands. Heavy and wide and kind. Could build a house
with those hands, could caress a woman, could fight
like a man, could make you stand up and believe in
something! Those hands. Magic, in those hands! Like
she could knock you out with one punch, make you feel
like a giant with one back slap, make a girl tremble and
moan with one stroke, make a crowd cry yes when she
raises her fist. Start a revolution with those fists! Start
a bar fight! Wipe my stupid tears and cuff my chin, tell
me I'm doing good kid, I'm doing good. Straighten my
tie, neaten my hair, hold me back for safety, nudge me
forward into courage. Her hands. Tender and honest,
brave and afraid, soft and solid and strong. Her hands.
The parents I never had. The god I never prayed to. She
sees me, really sees me, and loves me like a son. Like a
sun ray hazy sun daze day from yesterday that makes
her eyes drunk on nostalgia to remember today. Rebel
Dyke. Dark denim and stark white tee. Pretty mouth,
twinkly eyes, broad shoulders and big bold breasts.

Strong arms, strong neck, strong back, stand tall. Stand tall kid, stand tall!

23

(Written just for this collection. Call it Concrete Kisses *if it needs a title. Feel free to change pronouns for a closer fit to you.)*

I shoved her up against a metal railing fence, making it rattle and shake and scream into the night sky. Shoved her gently, kissed her hard. She ooofed this sound that signalled sex and I smirked into her mouth. I took her breath away, stole it away into my back pocket for the next grey rainy day when I'm not quite so confident. Not quite so cocky. Not quite so full of myself like I am this night, this night I'm so full I'm spilling over. Hands all over hungry for skin, desperately unbuckle untie unzip get these fucking clothes off. Girls' clothes are so complicated, who makes them so complicated? She laughs and takes my hand and drags me down the street. Heading to hers, head dizzy, legs heavy, boxers sticky. Tip back my head and sigh at the stars. Two a.m. and we're both high on life, high on lust fumes. Delicious delirious desire. Because in this moment I am all that I want to be and more. I am limitless expansion, reaching for the infinite, stretching so wide and so high I'm bursting at my seams.

Electric night of my dreams. I am swagger and sex in new jeans. This girl, this city. These concrete kisses.

24

(Written just for this collection. Call it Why Haven't You Text Back *if it needs a title. Feel free to change pronouns for a closer fit to you.)*

Middle of the night. Sticky twisted up sheets strangle this sweaty body pulsing with need. The phone screen inches from eyes, itchy and dry, and desperate. So desperate. Honestly, it's embarrassing, it's humiliating, but I still can't shift it. Jaw tight, teeth clenched, snap at the screen *why haven't you text back?!* As if saying it out loud will help. It doesn't. Phone lays stubbornly silent and my itchy thumbs threaten humiliation. No, don't do it don't! Type out something to be deleted. Type and delete. Type and delete. Type and delete. Scripting conversations that'll never happen because you haven't been learning your lines, have not been playing it right, missed all rehearsals, cameras rolling and you're not there. Haven't been turning up at all. How did I get this so wrong?! How did I misread your cues so spectacularly? Where the fuck is my self-respect?! And yet... Typed and sent... Sent? Oh god. /.. Oh god? Oh my fucking fuck fuck fuck god! /.. Desperate. Needy greedy sweat clingy cringey wanting you to want me no needing you to need me?! Promising myself over and over and over that I will *never* do this again, never never never again. But I'll just let myself just one last time just this one just one night. Keep my phone nearby. The light's too bright on these tired sad eyes but I keep it by my side just in case. Just in case it beeps, wishing and hoping though deep down knowing it won't. Because the girl of my dreams is asleep.

25

(Written just for this collection. Call it On the Train to Christmas *if it needs a title.)*

The night before Christmas Eve and I'm stuck on a slow train home to a hometown that is no longer home. To my family by origin, by blood, I guess. But certainly not by choice. Already dreading the awkward comments from aunts and uncles I only see twice a year and both times are a total shitshow. Dreading dad getting drunk and asking me to tell him exactly why it is I'm wearing that. Dreading mum crying into the washing up and refusing to sit down mum, just leave it! Dreading the Queen's Speech, and arguments about the monarchy. Dreading the casual racism, casual sexism, blatant homophobia and shocking transphobia over burnt roasties and lumpy gravy. I mean, really, why do we do it? It's seasonal self-harm wrapped up in Santa-printed paper. Oh how I long to sneak off somewhere sunny, a beach Christmas?! Oh yes! Or at least get an airbnb with some mates and float our way through the days on mushrooms and Bucksfizz. Oh God, can I just pause to say, that man opposite me? In the ill-fitted blue suit and cheap brown shoes. Never a good look. Never trust a man in brown shoes. Anyway, him? We hooked up last year, during Pride. He used a fake name and he hid me from his housemate. Really proud. He's got one pillow, and a hanging lightbulb, and dumbbells covered in dust. It was the saddest fuck I've, well actually that's not true but anyway. I've been eyeballing him for the last three stops, making him sweat. He's gonna, yep, he's moved to a different carriage. Fairplay. Good work on the boundaries babes. Anyway where was I, oh yeah Christmas, Shitmas. I mean, I really don't mean to sound ungrateful. I know I'm lucky to even have a family to hate. I just would like, at least once; to avoid chewy nut roast whilst holding space for other people's meat-eating guilt. To all the queers at Christmas, good luck huns!

26

(**CHLOE** *from* Bitch Boxer, *published originally by Bloomsbury, this speech has been significantly adapted for this collection.* Bitch Boxer *opened at the Edinburgh Fringe Festival in 2012, directed by Bryony Shanahan. The play enjoyed two sold-out runs at London's Soho Theatre and two National Tours. We returned to Edinburgh for the British Council Showcase before embarking on an International Tour.* Bitch Boxer *won the Soho Theatre Young Writers Award 2012, the Old Vic New Voices Edinburgh Season 2012, the British Council Showcase 2013, the Holden Street Theatre's Award 2013, the Clonmel Theatre Award 2014 and the Adelaide Fringe Award 2014. Enjoy the confessional, the colloquial, casual language to hide deep pain. Find the moments of lightness and the moments of absolute sincerity.)*

CHLOE. I've fucked it right up with Jamie. I got back from the gym. And Jamie's sat on the sofa, with this huge smile on his face. And I'm like, *'What's going on?'* And he's like, *'Nothing'.* And I'm like, *'What's going on?'* And he's like, *'Nothing'.* And I'm like, *'Well what you sat there smiling at then, you look like a nutter!'* And his smile gets bigger. And he goes, *'I got you sumfink'.* And it's a pair of trainers. Jamie's bought me a pair of trainers... And I can tell you're probably thinking, so fucking what? It's a pair of trainers, what's the problem, nobody died. Except that's exactly the point. You see, Len got me this book about grieving. And it's awful honestly, me and Jamie was proper cracking up laughing at it one night. I don't mean to be rude but yeah, it's like, really pathetic, all these sob stories and that. There's bit this woman wrote, about feeling like she was just floating along through her days, untethered, like she'd lost her feet. Which I found really fucking funny. Lost her feet. And I'm crackin' up laughing, when Jamie goes, *'Do you ever feel like that?' (Beat.)* No. *'If you ever do, just tell me yeah, I'll sort you out'.* Oh yeah? How you gonna do that then? *'Oh I'll think of sumink'. (Beat.)* So I'm standing there holding these trainers and he's staring at me, and I realise I've kinda fucked up a nice moment. Like this is meant to be all special and romantic and that. *'Don't you wanna try 'em on?'* Nah I say, in a minute. I wanna walk out but I curl up next to him on the sofa and bury my face in his chest. Lynx Africa fills my nose, I usually love that smell but now I just feel sick. He wraps his arms around me and kisses my head. Then he makes it worse by going, *'I know you're sad right now, cus of your dad. But you won't be forever, I promise. I love you Chloe. I'm gonna look after you'.* And I go to say sumink, you know, witty 'n clever, to lighten the mood and clear the air. But my throat closes up. I like, choke, on my words, and I'm trying my best to spit 'em out but it ain't happening. And cus I ain't said nothin' Jamie goes like, *'You do love me don't you Clo?' (Beat.)* When the girls asked what happened the only thing I can think to say, is to tell 'em that he bought me trainers. And people just don't get it. And I don't really know why I done it either, cus if I'm honest, it fucking hurts. Like, it was right there in front of me, he was offering me love in the form of some gold 'n white Nikes. And I'm thinking, go on Chloe, just put 'em on, go on I fucking dare ya, you deserve it, they're well nice! But I couldn't do it. Wouldn't have felt right. Like walking around with your shoes on the wrong feet. Dad always said footwork has to be spot on, you gotta *dance* Chloe.

27

*(**WOMAN ONE** from BLUSH, published originally by Bloomsbury. This speech has been significantly adapted for this collection. BLUSH was directed by Ed Stambollouian. BLUSH opened at the Edinburgh Fringe Festival 2016, before enjoying a run at London's Soho Theatre and a National Tour. BLUSH won the Underbelly Untapped Edinburgh Season 2016 and the Stage Edinburgh Award 2016. **WOMAN ONE** is a confident businesswoman whose younger sister is the recent victim of revenge pornography. She is trying to bottle her rage in this speech, trying to be articulate and not burst into tears. Enjoy the specificity. Let us see the struggle to stay in control, and let us see the mask slip sometimes.)*

WOMAN ONE. I'd like to take out each and every one of their eyeballs. Pluck them out, ever so gently and easily, with a precision and a grace that suggests I've done this a thousand times before. And by the end I will have, I'll have done it thirty thousand times. I'd like to place them, ever so gently, on the floor in neat little rows, all lined up next to each other like soldiers. I'd like to stand back and admire them, for a moment. The light shining off the cornea, fluid around the pupils gleaming like oyster pearls, like spilt egg yolk, like smokers' spit on concrete. I'd like to admire them, for a moment, thirty thousand pairs, strange in their beauty. An image I know will be branded tonight on the inside of my lids when I close my eyes to sleep. It's calming, looking at them sat patiently in their neat little lines, it's pleasing somehow, the regimented lines, the order, clinical and neat, it's pleasing to look at, somehow the precision is comforting.

I'd like to remove my shoes. And then I'd like to remove my socks. I want to be barefoot. It's *important* that I am barefoot, that my feet are, naked, that my skin can feel. The floor would be cold and that would, like the regimented lines, be somewhat somehow pleasing. I'm *pleased* the floor is cold, the temperature is correct somehow, it's comforting.

I would like to take a step, barefoot, towards the first pair of eyes. I would like to, slowly, without slipping off them, or knocking them out of line, I would like to slowly, stand on each one of those eyeballs. Stand on them barefoot. I want to be barefoot so I can feel each one strain under my weight, feel each one bulge under the arch of my foot as I apply more pressure, more weight, more of me, until the sweet surrender of its explosion under the skin of my foot. Its pop into non-existence squishing between my toes and oozing across the cold floor that's temperature is somehow comforting, the sound of each one popping is somehow comforting, thirty thousand pairs popped and I would somehow be comforted, and revenge would be had, and closure would be found, and peace would be restored and that, that is what I would like. *Very much.*

Thirty thousand. The number of views on the website. Thirty thousand, in what, twenty-four hours? My sister's only just eighteen. He was her first boyfriend, and she trusted him, and he thought it'd be funny. I want to smash his face in, I want to smash his face until there is nothing but bits of bloody bone, I've never felt such a terrible, fucking, *rage*. She says she feels like she's been raped. She says she feels like she's been raped thirty thousand times. She's just eighteen.

28

*(WOMAN TWO from BLUSH, published
originally by Bloomsbury. This speech has
been significantly adapted for this collection.
BLUSH was directed by Ed Stambollouian.
BLUSH opened at the Edinburgh Fringe
Festival 2016, before enjoying a run at
London's Soho Theatre and a National Tour.
BLUSH won the Underbelly Untapped
Edinburgh Season 2016 and the Stage
Edinburgh Award 2016. WOMAN TWO is a
party girl who thinks she's getting what she
wants, how she wants, when she wants it.
Working class and really sharp, politically
aware and smart. She could have made
a great lawyer or politician, if only she'd
stayed at school long enough to get the grades.
Enjoy the swagger and sass, but also let us
see glimpses of insecurity behind all that
front. This could be played by an actor of any
gender.)*

WOMAN TWO. He sent me a photo of his cock. Fully erect,
his sweaty palm pulling at it, the first bead of semen
sat glistening on the tip. I'm in Asda buying washing
detergent wondering if I really need non-bio. The bio
stuff is 64p cheaper. Vaguely remember having a rash
once, is that worth 64p? Beep and it's a text from him.
"R U Horny?" R. U. I hate it when people do that.
Missing letters really grate on me. I'm not even the best
at spelling but, yeah, no thanks. /.. Reply, 'yes', full stop.
Though the answer is obviously no. I'm in Asda.

And I mean, wow! The speed of his reply! It's both
astonishing and irritating as fuck. I mean if I text him
about anything, *anything* other than sex I'm left waiting
for *days*! Driving myself mad checking my phone a
thousand times?! Little blue screen's my night-light as

I lie awake waiting for him to love me. Phantom beeps interrupt my sleep, makes my desperate pathetic heart skip a beat then plummet back into the dark fucking depths of disappointment. And here, back here to the present, to Asda, to cold strip light and cold tile floor, I send a 'yes' and he replies instantly. With a photo of his cock. And I stare at it. And then I stare at the non-bio. Cock. Non-bio. Cock. Non-bio. Cock. Non-bio. Cock.

And praps it's cus I'm in Asda? Or praps I'm like getting numb to nudity? Or praps it's cus it's not a particularly nice image to look at, I mean they ain't very pretty, whatever, basically I feel *nothing*. Absolutely nothing? I feel the same way looking at the photo of his cock as I do looking at the non-bio. It's been at least ten seconds so he texts 'well'. Question mark. Dot. Dot. Dot.

I hold my thumb on the letter 'm' and click on some appropriate emojis. I dunno why. Hoping it'll make me feel something? Anything? I get the bio stuff. Skin might not like it but, a girl's gotta do what a girl's gotta do right?! And 64p ain't nothin' so *(Pats bum.)* that's Asda price.

29

(**DAUGHTER** *from* Pops, *published originally by Bloomsbury. This speech has been significantly adapted for this collection. Directed by Ali Pidsely and performed by the magic Sophie Melville, we opened at Edinburgh Fringe 2019 and also enjoyed a short run at HighTide's Adleburgh Festival.* Pops *won the HighTide Disruption Festival Edinburgh Season 2019 and The Stage Edinburgh Award 2019.* **DAUGHTER** *is a recovering addict, who's sober today by grit or grace or god. In this speech she's talking to her dad, who is not sober, and not easy to live with.*)

DAUGHTER. I put the washing on. Some of your underwear was in the pile. Your briefs. Blue. Your blue briefs. They had shit in them. Stains. Marks. Where you'd /.. Where you'd clearly /.. Tried to wipe /.. You'd shit yourself Dad. Poisoned yourself. Drank so much your body /.. I couldn't stop looking at it. Staring at it. The stain. And feeling so Terribly Angry at it. Which is daft really because it's not, Its fault is it? I mean it's just, what it is. A mark. A stain. But for me, looking at it I thought fuck, *fuck*! *Fucking hell!* That is, a very clear, a very Obvious Sign that you /.. That you're /.. And I thought about it being in the washing machine. The water and the soap lifting it, the particles of poo lifted off the fabric and floating around, getting stuck on the other clothes in the machine maybe, or maybe they'd wash away? The germs would? I mean it's hot isn't it, it's not like a quick rinse under a tap it's. Sixty fucking degrees, or forty or, depending on, eco fucking friendly and I /.. I thought about the particles getting stuck to my clothes. That's possible isn't it? A possible possibility of washing my clothes with *Your Shit Stain* is that some of it could. And I'd walk around with, Your Shit, stuck on me. And I'd ingest it. I'd breathe it in, get it stuck in my lungs. I'd be breathing your shit into my lungs. Carrying particles around with me on my clothes, seeping, into my skin into the pours in my, getting into my bloodstream, into my digestive system and maybe I'd be inspired by, Infected by you and it'd make me do the same. Kick off the desire to do the same and I'd Shit my pants, Shit you out sweet Sweet release Shit you out into my knickers and leave a forever Stain! ...Or maybe not. Maybe I'd carry you around inside me for *years*. Like chewing gum. How long is, seven years? ...I chucked 'em. Couldn't risk it. Couldn't risk the chance of turning into you. No, no! Don't say sorry, don't, don't you fucking dare. You, your sorrys don't mean shit you, you've run all out of sorrys. You've used them all up. You hear me? They're all gone for you, gone, all gone.

30

(**MAN ONE** *from* BLUSH, *published originally by Bloomsbury. This speech has been significantly adapted for this collection.* BLUSH *was directed by Ed Stambollouian.* BLUSH *opened at the Edinburgh Fringe Festival 2016, before enjoying a run at London's Soho Theatre and a National Tour.* BLUSH *won the Underbelly Untapped Edinburgh Season 2016 and the Stage Edinburgh Award 2016.* **MAN ONE** *is a young app designer who's dazzled by being in the spotlight after recent work success. Caught up in a whirlwind of attention,* **MAN ONE** *misreads a situation and tries to kiss a colleague. Humiliated, he gets drunk and it spills out into a public argument on twitter. Enjoy the movement opportunities here, and the dizzy high before the crashing low.)*

MAN ONE. Out with the boys! Who ask no questions, but seem to somehow understand, and I don't ask about their lives, their wives, no one asks why, it's just clear we all need this night. After three shots and two pints we declare we feel alive, and look at the lights! This night won't end in tears, this night we'll be loud, and lairy, and pretend we're not lonely, and do things we'll apologise for tomorrow morning. This night is The Night! This night is the same as every other fucking night but we'll do our best to pretend it isn't... On the dancer floor, probably embarrassing myself, but it's dark in here and, fuck it. I pull my phone out to, I dunno, swipe or click something, anything to avoid feeling my feelings. And I see she's tweeted. Some hashtag everyday sexism shit. I mean, raging. I am fucking raging. Making me out to look like /.. No way. And before I can stop it, I'm all furious thumbs. Ping. Sent! And it feels good for about two seconds. Ping Ping Ping! See people are agreeing with me. Ping ping ping! Alright lads easy. Oh /.. Oh shit /.. Oh shit I feel sick... Guilt wakes me in the morning. Guilt is in my mouth, lying thick and fuzzy on my teeth. All my organs feel dirty. I'm too scared to move in case something shatters so I lie still staring at the ceiling. My heart is beating fast. Too fucking fast! I think I'm dying and okay, okay it's okay you're okay, you're okay, okay roll over slowly and she's there. Shiny. Her light pulsing, laughing at me. No. No no no no no open it and check and yes, oh fuck, oh my fuck, I need to be sick.

9 780573 133657